I HAVE BEEN SHAMED ON THE INTERNET

NOW WHAT?

TAMRA B. ORR

ROSEN PUBLISHING®

New York

Published in 2017 by The Rosen Publishing Group, Inc.
29 East 21st Street, New York, NY 10010

Library of Congress Cataloging-in-Publication Data

Names: Orr, Tamra, author.
Title: I have been shamed on the Internet, now what? / Tamra
B. Orr.
Description: First edition. | New York : Rosen Publishing,
2017. | Series: Teen life 411 | Includes bibliographical refer-
ences and index.
Identifiers: LCCN 2016018733 | ISBN 9781508172024
(library bound)
Subjects: LCSH: Internet and teenagers—Juvenile literature.
| Humiliation—Juvenile literature. | Internet—Moral and
ethical aspects—Juvenile literature. | Online etiquette—
Juvenile literature.
Classification: LCC HQ799.2.I5 O77 2017 | DDC
004.67/80835—dc23
LC record available at https://lccn.loc.gov/2016018733

Manufactured in Malaysia

CONTENTS

The story captured worldwide attention. The cast of the tragedy included a beautiful teenage girl, a frustrated father, a personal photo, and the always open, never-ending internet.

On May 29, 2015, thirteen-year-old Izabel Laxamana jumped out of her grandmother's car as they crossed an overpass over Interstate 5 in Tacoma, Washington. She ran to the edge of the bridge and jumped, falling thirty feet onto the hood of a 2001 Nissan Altima going sixty-five miles an hour. The impact shattered the car's front and rear windshields. She died of her injuries the following day.

Why young Izabel committed suicide is still uncertain, but the links to internet shaming are unavoidable. The teen had been struggling for weeks. Her online posts stated she felt hated at school. Shortly before her death she posted, "In a school with so many people its weird to say 'i feel alone' but the truth is that you really do feel alone."

It all began the day Izabel decided to take a selfie. She donned a sports bra and leggings and sent the picture to a boy she liked. The boy shared the picture with friends. Soon the faculty found out about it. They contacted Izabel's parents. The Laxamanas didn't care for social media and had repeatedly warned their daughter to avoid it. If she didn't follow the rules, they warned, they'd cut off her long black hair.

Izabel had broken the rules, and Jeff Laxamana knew what had to be done. With a pair of scissors, he cut off all but one strand of her hair. Then he turned on the video camera and showed the pile of hair on the floor. "The consequences of getting messed up," he said in the fifteen-second video. "Man, you lost all that beautiful hair. Was it worth it?" Izabel whispered "no." The video ended soon after.

At school the next day, the video was spread from phone to phone. It didn't stop there. In the end, the video was seen more than four million times before being taken down. The school called child protective services. That following day, Izabel wrote eight farewell letters to family and friends. "In the notes, she [Izabel] explains that she did some things that were embarrassing, and she did not want to take the family name down with her," stated Loretta Cool, police spokeswoman from the Tacoma Police Department in an article by Natasha Norman for News.Mic.

As the young girl's death hit the news, fingers pointed at Jeff, Izabel's father. Clearly his video had pushed the young girl over the literal edge, people yelled. Others petitioned he lose his job, and many insisted he be arrested. Ultimately, no charges were filed, but the Laxamana family was still vilified, even while coping with the loss of their child.

In the end, after all the rumors and false information, it turned out that while the father did cut his daughter's hair and film it, he never uploaded the video to the internet. Someone else in what the police called "a tragically misguided attempt to help correct the teen's behavior" did it. Cool stated the father's decision to film the moment was so that Izabel would think twice before ever posting another selfie. "It was part of the discipline process," Cool explained.

A young girl is dead and who is to blame? Was it her fault for betraying her parents' rules? Was it the boy who shared her selfie or the person who uploaded the video? Was it the father's discipline method? Or was it the internet—that worldwide communication network that turns local rumors into global truths in a matter of seconds?

Shame is an extremely powerful feeling and one that can easily connect to depression, anger, and many other destructive emotions.

A Modern Scarlet Letter

Shame.

It has been a part of humanity since the first people walked the planet.

According to the Merriam-Webster Dictionary, shame is "a feeling of guilt, regret, or sadness that you have because you know you have done something wrong." It plays a role in everyone's life but is also one of the best ways people learn essential life lessons.

Shame is what makes kids learn not to steal when they take that first candy bar when Mom is not looking, but get caught when munching on it in the car. Shame is what makes little ones more careful when playing in the house because Grandma's lamp just shattered in the living room. Shame is what makes teens do their chores when they realize that by not doing them, they are creating more work for someone else in the family. Shame is what convinces young people to study harder when they get caught cheating on a test. In other words, shame often makes people behave better because they see how their mistakes lead to

Knowing you have done something wrong is often painful, but it can also be the key to making changes and improvements.

Bullying and shaming is not only done face to face but also through various social media sites. Hurtful messages can be as close as your cell phone.

getting in trouble or upsetting someone, often someone they care about.

Shame is found in all kinds of literature. Look at fairy tales: the ugly duckling is ridiculed and made to feel shame for his appearance; Cinderella is humiliated by her haughty stepsisters and stepmother; poor Rudolph and his red nose are mocked by other reindeer. In each case, shame teaches an important lesson. So—is shame a good thing? Maybe.

Internet shaming is a problem that appears to be growing almost at the same speed as the internet itself. Using social media to target a person and then humiliate him or her has taken on an almost vigilante mentality.

People make accusations, and then act as judge and jury before all of the facts—or *any* of the facts—are in. What was just a piece of gossip or a story a moment ago might be reported and then forwarded again and again as fact. Cyberbullying, or going online to intimidate, threaten, or bully someone, is part of this whole internet trend.

What makes internet shaming truly dangerous, however, is its reach. Where a few decades ago, a rumor might be restricted to a school and its students and staff, today, it is not restricted at all. That gossip can be on the other side of the planet within an hour—or less. People's reputations can be damaged—or ruined. People's lives can be injured, or, as in the case of Izabel Laxamana, they can come to a tragic end.

In the past, shame was limited to the people nearby. For example, people who had broken laws or done something to be ashamed of might be put into stocks or flogged right in the middle of the village. They were examples to others to not make the same mistake. Villagers could come by and mock the person, often silently being grateful that it was not their hands and heads locked into the wooden frame or their backs being cut to ribbons.

Nathaniel Hawthorne explored the idea of shame in his classic novel, *The Scarlet Letter*. The novel was published in 1850, and takes place in Puritan Boston in the

In this illustration, Prynne is being led to the pillory so that her shame and her punishment can be seen by everyone.

Today's teens know how to send messages in multiple ways, spreading news—and rumors—faster than anyone could have imagined a decade ago.

1600s, a time of strict morals and harsh punishment. In the novel, the main character, Hester Prynne, is charged with adultery. In addition to serving a sentence in prison, she is also forced to wear a red "A" on her chest while standing in the town square. Her ongoing shame is used as a lesson to others to not follow Prynne's immoral example.

FROM LOCAL SCANDAL TO GLOBAL DISGRACE

Whether it is characters in stories or just regular people throughout time, everyone makes mistakes (or actions that some perceive as mistakes). Everyone feels guilty and deals

THE NEW STOP, DROP, AND ROLL

Lisa France is the senior producer for CNN Digital's Entertainment section. She offers a number of short videos with helpful advice about the internet. In her ninety-second video about internet shaming, she advises everyone to "Stop, Drop, and Roll" when it comes to sharing information on the internet. "If you're going to share something with a friend that looks outrageous, or even if it doesn't look outrageous, I need you to stop, drop, and roll. Stop before you hit that share button, drop on over to Google, and roll around in the information that you find out over there. I'm just looking out for you," France continues. "You make yourself look crazy when you post this stuff."

with shame. It is a common, time-worn condition. However, one element has changed dramatically over the years. Where once these incidents would have been local situations, today they are international news. (As one popular saying goes, "I'm so glad I was young and stupid before camera phones.")

In seconds, a story of someone's mistake, careless comment, embarrassing photo, or highly personal video can be leap frogging from city to state, state to country, country to continent as people share and pass it on. It is easy to see why the internet has been labeled "a weapon of mass reputation destruction."

How can images uploaded to a friend's Facebook page turn into forty thousand hits on YouTube in a matter of hours? It helps to keep in mind that teens spend a huge amount of time on social media every day. In fact, a 2015 report by Common Sense Media stated that U.S. teens spend about nine hours a day using media of some kind. Nine hours. That is more time than they spend sleeping, sitting in class, or being with family. "It just shows that these kids live in this massive 24/7 digital media technology world, and it's shaping every aspect of their life," stated James Steyer, chief executive officer and founder of Common Sense Media, to Kelly Wallace in an article for CNN. "They spend far more time with media technology than any other thing in their life. This is the dominant intermediary in their life." This dedication to social media outlets means sharing, passing, and creating stories and images over and over.

STORIES IN THE HEADLINES

The stories of internet shaming are often splashed all over the news. One of the most telltale indications of this type of incident is that it spreads fast, and the details being reported are not always entirely accurate. Sometimes the person being crucified online is at fault, and sometimes he or she is nothing but a victim. Sometimes the person made an offhand remark that turned into disaster, thanks to the internet, and sometimes a momentary lapse in judgment becomes a haunting action with ripple effects. Just ask Adam, Justice, Lindsey, or Adria.

Adam Mark Smith was the CFO of a medical device company in Arizona. Then, like many other people across the United States, in summer of 2012, he was upset by the company Chick-fil-A's stance on homosexuality. He decided he wanted to protest, so he made a plan. He drove to a local restaurant and went through the drive-thru to order a free cup of water. As he did, he filmed himself giving the drive-thru's employee a hard time about the company. "Chick-fil-A is a hateful corporation," he said to the attendant according to an article by Joseph Diaz and Lauren Effron. "I don't know how you live with yourself and work here. I don't understand it. This is a horrible corporation with

When Chick-fil-A's CEO Dan Cathy made a public remark on his company's support of traditional marriage, the sparks begin flying—and people like Adam Smith began speaking out.

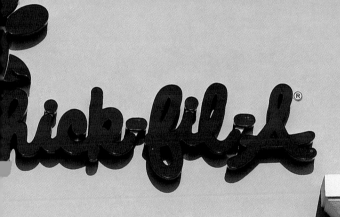

Smartphones make it a snap to photograph or take a video and post it online. But as Adam Mark Smith found out, careful consideration before posting is crucial.

horrible values. You deserve better." Smith posted his video to his personal YouTube channel and then went back to work feeling pleased he had spoken out. To his amazement, when he got to work, his secretary told him that the company's voice mail was completely full and even included some bomb threats.

Smith was fired immediately. Within days, death threats were sent to his home. The address of his children's school was released to the public. He lost his job and his home. He and his wife and four children had to move. He made an online apology to the drive-thru attendant and was forgiven, but it did not make any difference. The damage was done. Smith has continued looking for work, but as soon as potential

MYTHS AND FACTS

MYTH:

Before anything is published on the internet, it has been thoroughly fact-checked.

FACT:

Even the best news sites sometimes miss fact-checking information in the rush to be the first to report something, so chances are posts from friends or people that you have 'friended' have not done any research on the validity of what they are sharing. Consider it all with skepticism and doubt. If the information is about an event or well-known person, check out the sites BreakTheChain.org, TruthOrFiction.com, or Snopes.com to get the real facts.

MYTH:

If I post something online and then change my mind and delete it, it is gone.

FACT:

It is much, much harder to remove information from the internet than most people think. There are techniques posted—where else?—online that guide you through it, but never rely on just the edit or delete buttons to take care of it. And never assume that just because you deleted your original post, the information hasn't already been re-tweeted and forwarded by countless others.

MYTH:

Posting something stupid today is not going to have any effect on me in the future.

FACT:

Because what you post online has the potential to go anywhere in the world and last indefinitely, a revealing photo, a stupid comment, or a drunk post can be seen by future partners, employers, and landlords (to name a few). That silly forgotten post may result in not getting that date, job, or apartment.

MYTHS AND FACTS

employers find out he is *that* guy, the interview is over. "I think people are scared," Smith said. "I think people are scared that it could happen again." Currently, Smith and his family are living on food stamps, and he has written a book about his experience titled *A Million Dollar Cup of Water: Discovering the Wealth in Authenticity.*

In 2013, Justine Sacco was taking a long trip from New York to South Africa. The senior director of a corporate communications company, she was used to traveling. As she made the trip, she tweeted about her experience, from difficult airplane passengers to long layovers. Her last tweet was "Going to Africa. Hope I don't get AIDS. Just kidding, I'm white!"

Sacco slept for most of the eleven-hour flight from London to Cape Town. When she landed and turned her cell phone back on, she was shocked to see it being flooded with texts and alerts. When her best friend Hannah called, Sacco answered. "You're the No. 1 worldwide trend on Twitter right now," she informed the baffled Sacco. While Sacco's plane crossed the planet, the internet world had exploded with fury over her perceived racist message. One of the tweeted responses was from her employer. "This is an outrageous, offensive comment," they wrote. Sacco received death threats and rape threats. ". . . but it wasn't trolls who destroyed her, it was good people like us," writes Jon Ronson in his book *So You've Been Publicly Shamed.* "It was nice people, empathetic people trying to do good. It was hundreds of thousands of empathetic people, that's what destroyed

Justine Sacco, robbing her joke of nuance and just trying to destroy her . . ."

When Sacco arrived in Cape Town, she found out she was unemployed. The next few days were a nightmare. "I cried out my body weight in the first twenty-four hours," she said. "It was incredibly traumatic. You don't sleep. You wake up in the middle of the night forgetting where you are. . . I had a great career, and I loved my life, and it was taken away from me . . . " she added. Attempting to salvage her life, Sacco rarely discusses what happened to her with anyone. "Anything that puts the spotlight on me is a negative," she said.

Lindsey Stone and her coworker Jamie had a fun tradition going. They would find street signs and the take pictures or videos of themselves doing the opposite of what the signs stated. "No Smoking" signs had them lighting up cigarettes, for example. So when Stone was visiting Arlington National Cemetery's Tomb of the Unknowns and saw a sign saying, "Silence and Respect," she saw the perfect photo opportunity. She squatted down, and pretended to scream while raising her middle finger. Her friend took the picture and uploaded it to Stone's Facebook page.

A month went by before the repercussions of Stone's photo hit the internet. Someone spotted the photo and started sharing it online. By the next day, there was a "Fire Lindsey Stone" Facebook page. Reporters surrounded the woman's home. When she went to work at a center for developmentally disabled adults, she was told she no longer worked there. For the next year, Stone rarely left home. She was grappling with depression and insomnia. "I didn't want to be seen by anyone," she admitted to author Jon Ronson in an article for *The New York Times Magazine*. "I didn't want people looking at me."

In 2013, Adria Richards was sitting at a technology conference in California when she overheard two men talking behind her. They were discussing a computer or mobile device attachment called a dongle. One of the men, known only as "Hank" in order to retain his anonymity, shared a joke with his friend. "It was so bad I don't remember the exact words," he told Jon Ronson in an article for *The Guardian*. "It was about a fictitious piece of hardware that has a really big dongle—a ridiculous dongle. We were giggling about that. It wasn't even conversation-level volume." Richards, sure that the joke they were making was sexual and derogatory stood up and took a photo of the two men. She posted it on Twitter with the comment, "Not cool. Jokes about . . . 'big' dongles. Right behind me." A matter of minutes later, Hank and his friend were removed from the conference and asked to explain their remarks. The next day, Hank was fired. "I packed up all my stuff in a box," he told Ronson. "I went outside to call my wife. I'm not one to shed tears, but . . . when I got in the car with my wife I just . . . I've got three kids. Getting fired was terrifying."

The story didn't end with Hank's firing, however. When he posted what happened to him online, the anger shifted over to Richards. She was bombarded with death threats on Facebook and Twitter. Her home address was published online. She left her house out of fear of being attacked. Her employer's website was hacked and she was fired. As Ronson quoted Richards in his book, "I cried a lot during this time, journaled, and escaped by watching movies," she said. "I felt betrayed. I felt abandoned. I felt ashamed. I felt rejected. I felt alone."

In each one of these cases, a person had a momentary error in judgment, sharing personal opinions, making a flippant remark, or doing something for fun on the internet, and forgetting that the world could read and see them, and then condemn them for the crime of being human. They made a mistake and then, like Hester Prynne, these people, and many more, are forced to stand in front of a harsh and judgmental crowd. Only this time the crowd is the world, and they always seem to be in a severely punishing mood. There is often no forgiveness here, just a type of emotional mob justice, often with devastating results.

CHAPTER 2

INTERNET MOB JUSTICE

Twitter. Facebook. Vine. Instagram. There is no doubt that the internet is always finding new ways for you and your friends to connect and communicate. It might be a quick post, a seconds-long video, or a silly photograph. In less than a minute, friends know where others are, what they are doing, whom they are with, and what they are thinking. This world of instant messages and constant sharing is so common that it is today's norm, but it is not without its flaws. One of those flaws is people's tendencies to use the internet not to communicate, but to condemn.

It is far too easy for the people who pass on rumors, share illicit photos, or comment on intimate videos to forget one thing: behind the gossip and the images is a person with feelings and family. It's much easier to laugh and ridicule the person if those facts are overlooked, but it doesn't change them. Perhaps that person made an error in judgment. He drank more

Sharing a message or photo is only one click away with most smartphones. It makes keeping in touch simple, but it also makes shaming just as simple.

"For the Lulz": Trolls and Online Shaming

With the rise of internet culture, another phenomenon has come about known as "trolling." Trolls are internet users who intentionally disrupt, upset, or provoke other users. While trolling began as a relatively harmless practice, over time trolling has become more aggressive. It often aims to embarrass or cause real distress to other users on social media or message boards. Trolling often takes pranking to a hurtful and extreme level. It is motivated by humor at the expense of others.

Certain websites are well known for their culture of trolling. Perhaps most notable is the /b/ message board on the popular forum 4chan. In an August 2008 article, *The New York Times* described this message board as "the inside of a high-school bathroom stall or an obscene telephone party line." The ability to make anonymous posts allows users to post highly offensive content without repercussions. Other users might feel like they have little recourse to put an end to such behavior.

Wherever they appear on the web, trolls operate under the premise that the greater distress they can cause another user, the greater their own pleasure. This pleasure is measured in "lulz," a term derived from the common acronym "lol" that denotes the laughter trolls get from shaming another person online. Users need to be aware of cyber trolls. Avoid forums where trolling occurs and report or block users who post offensive content. While other users may do it "for the lulz," online shaming is never funny.

than he should have and ended up allowing pictures to be taken. She trusted the person she was with so much that she posed intimately for him. Or perhaps the people being intentionally humiliated are not even aware that a camera is pointed at them. It is being done without any of their knowledge at all.

One of the types of internet shaming that has developed over the past few years is "slut shaming." Slut shaming is the act of criticizing any young woman for her real—or presumed real—sexual activities. Often this type of shaming is done by taking pictures or videos of any female involved in sexual activity and sharing it, without permission, on the internet. Unfortunately, this type of shaming often ends up creating frightened, confused, desperate young men and women.

SLUT SHAMING

In summer 2012, fifteen-year-old Audrie Pott told her mother she was going to spend the night at a friend's house, but instead, she went to a party. While there, she drank so much she ended up passing out in a bedroom. When she woke up, most of her clothes were off. Her body had been written on and colored with Sharpies®— and she remembered absolutely nothing about any of it.

While Audrie was unconscious, three classmates she had known for years sexually assaulted her and used permanent markers to write crude remarks all over her. Everything was captured on the boys' cell phones. Once Audrie woke up, she immediately started asking

Larry and Lisa Pott's organization focuses on honoring their daughter by helping others who might be struggling with the pain of bullying and shaming.

questions about what had happened. When she had pieced it all together, she pleaded with one of the boys to destroy the pictures he and his friends had taken. Instead, he shared them with classmates. She was teased and taunted at school. According to Julia Prodis Sulek in an article in the *San Jose Mercury News*, Pott wrote on her Facebook page, "I have a reputation for a night I don't even remember and the whole school knows." Eight days after that post, Audrie came home from school, went into her bathroom, and hanged herself.

The three teen boys who assaulted Audrie were eventually arrested and convicted. Because of their ages at the time of the crime (fifteen and sixteen years old), they were given light jail sentences ranging from thirty to forty-five days. Soon after, Audrie's parents filed a wrongful-death lawsuit against two of the boys and their families and, in April 2015, they won the case. Part of the settlement determined that the boys had to apologize for their actions, as well as give ten presentations at high schools and youth groups about the dangers of drinking alcohol, taking nude photos, and "slut shaming." One of the teens, Christopher High, stated how sorry he was for his actions. "This has caused tragedy to all involved due to my actions. I will do everything I can to mentor teens to not do what I did . . ."

Today Audrie's parents run the Audrie Pott

Posting inappropriate photos of others without their knowledge or permission is more than just mildly embarrassing. It can have long-lasting or even fatal consequences for the victim.

Shame is a challenging emotion to handle in the first place, but when it is combined with an audience, it becomes dangerous.

Foundation (blog.audriepott-foundation.com) to provide anti-cyberbullying presentations to schools, as well as art and music scholarships and grants for school therapists. As the website states, "It is only fitting that her [Audrie's] passing could become a catalyst for change and that the positive and beautiful life she led would continue in her absences to provide a glimmer of hope and love in this world." Audrie's story is also part of a documentary film called *Audrie & Daisy*, released in 2016.

In March 2011, another young girl lost her life only hours after finding out that a video of her being forced to perform a sex act on a boy was being passed around school. Chevonea Kendall-Bryan, a thirteen-year-old living in London, England,

When "I'm Sorry" Isn't Enough

You made a mistake. You posted something or passed along something that ended up being hurtful as well as untrue. So now what?

An apology is often the first step. Just stepping up, admitting you made an error, and then sincerely expressing your regrets is a good place to start. The apology must be genuine, however. "You should never attempt an apology because someone else tells you it is the right thing to do, because the person is expecting it or because it will get you what you want," said Beverly Engle, author of *The Power of Apology*. "Apologies that are used as manipulations or mere social gestures will come across as empty and meaningless."

Instead, according to Engle, a meaningful apology should include three basic elements: regret, responsibility, and remedy. By showing genuine regret, you show that you recognize your actions were hurtful. By taking responsibility, you demonstrate that you are not making an excuse for what you did or putting the blame on someone else. Finally, by offering to remedy a situation, you emphasize that you want to help solve the problem, even if it is only to promise you that you will not repeat the behavior.

Unfortunately, there are times when an apology is simply not enough to solve the problem. What can you do then? Experts suggest that you continue to role model the behavior you wish you had adopted before (i.e., no more unfounded or unkind posts online), and get involved in educating and helping others to better understand the effect of internet shaming on people's lives. Perhaps, by your actions and life changes, you will help others understand that some mistakes are too big to be fixed by an apology. By realizing this, there is hope that they will avoid making these kinds of errors and causing someone else pain and tragedy.

You've been taught to say, "I'm sorry" since you were a little kid. The key to an apology, however, is that it is sincere and heartfelt—not just words.

had been bullied for years by a number of boys in school. According to an interview with one of Chevonea's friends conducted by Louise Eccles and Claire Ellicott of the *Daily Mail*, "It started off verbal, then physical, then cyberbullying. It never stopped for a few months or a few weeks—it was at least every day there was some kind of bullying happening." Although Chevonea, her friends, and even her mother went to teachers and school administrators for help, they were told that this was normal behavior for boys and that sometimes kids can be cruel.

On a spring afternoon, Chevonea stood on the window ledge of her fourth-floor home and begged the boy standing below to remove the video of her from his phone. Seconds later, she fell to the sidewalk. Bernard Richmond, a London coroner, told the *Daily Mail* that he believed that she fell, rather than jumped. In her court case, he testified, "I am satisfied that Chevonea felt so desperate and hopeless that, at about 8 p.m., she decided to do something dramatic to try and force E6 [the young man] into doing what she wanted." Richmond believed that the young girl lost her balance and fell, but not everyone agreed with this ruling.

MOB JUSTICE

In so many cases of internet shaming, you, a person—human, flawed, and vulnerable—made a mistake or simply showed an error in judgment. Often it's just a casually said comment made to entertain or make your friends laugh. Other times it's opening yourself up to risk and danger by losing control. Sometimes it is trusting another person too much and too fast. Or, as in the case of Chevonea, it's being pressured and bullied into doing something you did not want to.

It sounds like the bad name of an X-rated movie, but revenge porn refers to the "sharing of sexually explicit photos or videos of another person without that person's consent." Another name for it is "non-consensual pornography." A person may have originally agreed to have personal photos taken while in the nude or having sexual sessions recorded, but what happens if the couple breaks up and suddenly those images are put on the internet? That person may become a victim of revenge porn. An angry ex-partner may upload those images simply to embarrass or humiliate an individual, although sometimes they do it just for "fun" or to get attention or gain popularity. Unfortunately, this private information can reach employers, friends, and even family members, and sometimes contains the person's personal contact information as well.

Since 2014, it has been against the law to publish a private sexual image of another identifiable person without his or her consent. This includes images on the internet, as well as those shared via text and email. Currently twenty-seven states in the United States have laws against revenge porn. If convicted, a person can serve as much as two and a half years in prison, plus pay a fine.

REVENGE PORN LEGISLATION

In internet shaming, however, those human errors are punished severely. Instead of a lecture from mom and dad, a week's worth of grounding, or a month of lost privileges, young people are being humiliated in a wider and wider arena. Online users who laugh, point, and immediately go on to share are imposing impossibly harsh sentences on these minute mistakes. They are taking people who may or may not have made the smallest error and treating them with viral rage and righteous indignation. In the process, they are ruining and even ending too many lives.

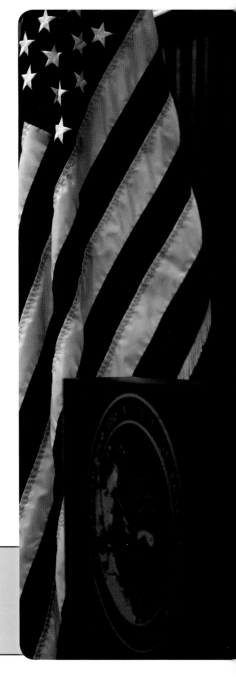

Attorney general Kamala D. Harris discusses the case of Kevin Bollaert, who posted revenge porn, or "sextortion" images. He asked the victims to pay to have the humiliating photos removed.

CHAPTER 3

"Teaching You a Lesson": Parental Shaming

Jeff Laxamana will most likely never forget how filming his daughter's shame helped contribute to losing her forever. Unfortunately, a number of parents haven't figured out this lesson yet.

Parental shaming, or using the internet to discipline a child through humiliation is a frightening new trend. Whenever a child makes a mistake, or does something that his or her parents have expressly forbidden—from acting up in the classroom to taking selfies and sending them to friends—it can be a frustrating experience. Parents usually set rules for reasons, and when these rules are broken, parents frequently feel the need to reinforce those lessons with the right kind of discipline. What qualifies as the proper kind, however, is constantly up for debate.

What happens when the idea of discipline slides over into punishment? Worst of all, what happens when that punishment meets online exposure? Discipline should be a private matter between parent and child. It should be designed to help the young person find a better

One of the responsibilities of parenting in discipline, but when discipline is combined with the internet, it is more than a lesson. It is punishment.

Conflict between parents and kids is normal, and figuring out how to reconcile is tricky. It becomes much more difficult if that conflict is shared with the public.

path, make a better choice, select a better direction. It should not be entertainment and fodder for the online masses to watch and comment on, while young people writhe in shame and mortification.

DISCIPLINE VERSUS PUNISHMENT

Parenting isn't easy. It calls for patience, wisdom, and constant decision making. One of the most complex parts of parenting is discipline. Discipline is done in order to help children make smarter, safer choices. It teaches lessons about proper ways to behave in today's society. It does not involve pain or fear, but rather the idea of consequences.

On the other hand, punishment is used to control behavior. It typically is a physical punishment, although many parents may use emotional or mental methods as well. As Jeannie Cunnion, author of *Parenting the Wholehearted Child* wrote for Sam Judah of Fox News, "Punishment is directed at the personhood of the child, and discipline is directed at the behavior that the child has displayed." Discipline helps a child learn how to change, while punishment introduces children to shame.

With the birth of the internet, a number of parents have found a new way to shame their children as part of their discipline methods. Do as you

Parents sometimes react emotionally to their teen's complaints and objections, but it's as important for them to stop for a deep breath before responding as it is for young people.

have been told, or suffer the consequences, which can be shared with the entire world. This method is almost universally rejected by experts in child development. Norma Simon, a psychologist, told *Time* magazine, ". . . whether or not you believe shaming a child is wrong, it usually doesn't work as a deterrent. . . . The reaction to shame is an inherent sense that you're no good, that you're damaged as a person. And if you're no good," she added, "what hope do you have of correcting what's going on?"

The lesson about changing behavior isn't learned with punishment, especially when done online. Instead, the message may end up being "you're a bad kid, so why change?"

Parents who succumb to posting their discipline methods online usually do for one reason: they cannot think of what else to do to teach these lessons. "Some people think these parents are evil, but they're not," said Simon. "They're desperately trying to solve a problem, even if their solution is damaging." The problem is, despite their intentions, using public shame to teach a lesson is definitely damaging. "I think it would be difficult to find someone in the field of psychology and mental health who would say [public child shaming] is appropriate," child psychologist Karyl McBride told BBC Trending. "When parents are

Young people are sometimes bullied and shamed by their peers, so it is especially stressful when the shaming continues at home.

shaming and humiliating children that impacts the child's ability to have proper bonding and attachment with those parents. It impairs trust," she said. "It causes the children to grow up with internal messages of 'I'm a bad person.' And that's not going to develop a healthy human being."

EVERYDAY SHAME

Despite this evidence, parental shaming is happening every day—and is often praised in public as a valid and effective method of discipline. In 2015, Valerie Sparks shamed her thirteen-year-old daughter for stating she was nineteen years old on her Facebook profile and posing in a bra and panties. In an online video, she forces her daughter to stand on screen and explain she was lying, despite the daughter's obvious distress and tears. "Don't cry now," she told BuzzFeed's Stephanie McNeal. "You wasn't crying when you was posting pictures on Facebook, was you? In a bra? Some little girl in some lace panties that you know you don't own. You still wear panties that say Monday, Tuesday, Wednesday." Sparks was praised for protecting her daughter from possible online sexual predators—a valid concern but one that could have perhaps been addressed in a gentler way out of the public eye.

Love, patience, and compassion are often the keys to solving conflicts between parents and teens. The internet does not need to have any part in the communication.

STOP SHAMING CHILDREN

Robbyn Peters Barnett is a child mental-health specialist who works with kids who have suffered from abuse and neglect. In an opinion piece for the *Seattle Times*, she wrote, "It is one thing to commiserate with the frustrations of parenting, it is another to promote a parent's worst fear, 'Yes, your child deserves to be humiliated.' Never trust a mob with someone you love, especially your child. Consider what happens to a child who watches their picture float around the internet with an ovation of applause for their parents' cruelty. Look at the blank, zoned-out expression on their faces. I see pain, humiliation and hatred," she continued. "Even more disturbing, sometimes I see nothing. The child has drifted away. Shame is an enduring experience that can last a lifetime. It plants the seed, 'Who I am is bad.' For some, like the young girl whose father forcefully cut off her hair, the shame was so unbearable that suicide felt like her only option. Suicide—the ultimate act of shame."

Barnett and other professionals have established the StopShamingKids.com campaign. It includes a petition that addresses the issue of parental shaming and asks everyone to reach out and help put an end to it today (available at http://www.teach-through-love.com/stop-shaming-kids.html).

1. How can my text or email end up on the internet?

2. How can I respond to being shamed on the internet?

3. How do I delete or take down something posted on the internet?

4. What can my school do to help with the problem of internet shaming?

5. Do my parents have a legal right to shame me online?

6. Why do people want to humiliate or embarrass me?

7. How can I take back something I've posted or said online?

8. Is it legal for someone to Photoshop my face on a sexually graphic picture?

9. My ex-boy/girlfriend has nude photos of me. How can I get them back?

10. I know someone who is being shamed online. What can I do to help or make it stop?

10 GREAT QUESTIONS
TO ASK A SCHOOL COUNSELOR

In 2012, North Carolina father Tommy Jordan got angry when he discovered his teenage daughter had posted a negative comment about having to do chores on her Facebook page. It was an emotional post that wasn't quite as well thought out as it could have been—in other words, a teenager's rant about life. Jordan's solution? He filmed his own eight-minute rant and then pulled out a 45-caliber handgun and shot his daughter's laptop nine times. He uploaded the film, called "Facebook Parenting: For the Troubled Teen," to YouTube and soon amassed millions of views. The police and Child Protective Services came to see Jordan after the incident, and both were fine with his method of parenting. Two years after the incident, Jordan stands by how he handled the situation. "My daughter acted up on Facebooks—what my mom would have called 'in front of God and everybody.' So I responded in front of God and everybody," he said according to a Huffington Post article by Ryan Buxton.

While many hailed Jordan as a parenting hero, many others were appalled that he chose such a public and violent way to discipline his daughter. Had the computer been his wife's and Jordan had done the same thing, would it have been seen as discipline? Others wondered why Jordan didn't shoot the laptop in front of his daughter rather than in front of a camera. Who was the lesson

Even if the intention is to instruct and teach, some lessons made public on the internet may do more harm than good.

intended for? As one psychiatrist posted posted in he article "The Father that Shot His Daughter's Computer." on his bog, ". . . both of the dummies involved [in the incident] violated one of the cardinal rules of family: don't disparage someone in the family to someone outside the family."

The stories don't end there. Parents are putting signs around their children's necks detailing their mistakes and putting them online. They're forcing their children to say they lied, stole, or failed a test and posting the videos on YouTube. They are having their children stand in the middle of the city where traffic can honk and yell at them for acting up in class or twerking at a school dance. They're taking a private issue that should be discussed personally with love and patience and making it a sideshow for people to watch, and spread throughout the planet at will. Instead of being their children's allies, these parents seem to be their adversaries. This type of punishment is often put under the heading of "for your own good," but as multiple experts are trying to point out, this is not helping young people. It may be teaching lessons—but not the right ones, and it is definitely not for anyone's "good."

Rachel Stafford, author of *Hands Free Mama,* told Rebekah Lowin of "Today," "A lot of the time, we respond to our children in ways that really don't reflect a connection or a nurturing because we're trying to teach them a lesson. We belittle them. It's imperative that we ask ourselves, 'Is this something that will embarrass my child when they get older? Is this something I really need the world to see?'" she added. "And, you know, the truth is, it doesn't matter whether it's cute or funny or shaming and cruel. It really comes down to the same couple of questions."

CREATING CHANGE

Wayman Gresham had heard a great deal about parental shaming, and he was ready to get involved. In a video that has been seen at least twenty million times online, he towers over his son with an electric razor. "I'm going to teach my son a lesson," he said. Before a single cut is made, however, Gresham says, "Wait a minute. Come here boy, give me a hug." This anti-shaming video was Gresham's way to admonish parents for using this method for teaching their children. "I've gone on Facebook and many times I've seen this kind of punishment, cutting off the hair or a child being embarrassed one way or another," Gresham told Sam Judah of the BBC. "There is no legitimate reason for humiliating your child, there is no legitimate reason for snatching their dignity away. . . . Nevertheless, to get on Facebook and humiliate your child like this, it's not for the benefit of the child. The overall message is, we could all do better as parents."

Dr. Shefali Tsabary, clinical psychologist and author of *The Conscious Parent* is vehemently against public shaming of children. "I had been seeing these shaming videos online for years, and I'd always found them to be stomach-turning," she said. She created two videos about parental shaming, along with a petition that garnered more than thirty thousand signatures. Her movements are called #ENDSHAME and #CREATECONNECTIONS. "It really comes from this idea of parents thinking they can control their children, and thinking that children can only learn through shame," she said. Although her videos contain some painful and graphic videos of shamed children, Dr. Tsabary feels it is necessary to include them. "I'm not trying to scandalize or get stuck looking at these images. I'm trying to use them as a springboard from which we can understand and bring attention to a tough issue."

CHAPTER 4

THE WEIGHT OF SHAME

Anger. Happiness. Sadness. Frustration. Amusement. Depression. Anxiety. Shame.

Most emotions come and go on a daily, even hourly basis. Emotions are just a normal part of life—especially young people's lives. In part, they are caused by fluctuating hormones and a still developing brain, but can also be a result of dealing with constant pressure from school, friends, and family.

While shame is often thought of as an emotion, it is one that is different than most of the other emotions. It tends to have a stronger and more long-lasting impact on people's lives. It has far more weight.

Psychologist Carl Jung once said, "Shame is a soul eating emotion." He was right. Shame tends to inspire a number of other devastating and dangerous emotions such as depression and anger. As Dr. Mary Lamia wrote in her article "Shame: A Concealed, Contagious, and Dangerous Emotion" for *Psychology Today*, " Given that shame can lead you to feel as though your whole self is flawed, bad, or subject to exclusion, it makes you want to withdraw or hide yourself."

Shame is like the first in a long line of dominos. Once it tips over, other negative emotions and actions can too easily follow.

One of shame's most lethal components is what other emotions it can drag along. Dr. Lamia wrote, "In addition to the many emotions that can accompany shame, such as envy, anger, rage, and anxiety, we can also include the affects [sic] of sadness, depression, depletion, loneliness, and emptiness as a result. And this is where shame can become a dangerous emotion. When shame is experienced as overwhelming, it can negatively color how you view yourself and how you assess the prospect of recovering your self-esteem."

It can be easy to confuse the emotions of shame and guilt, but the two are not the same at all. Guilt focuses on a behavior, while shame focuses on a person. If a teen shoplifts a t-shirt

#DONTJUDGEMECHALLENGE VERSUS #BEAUTYINALLCHALLENGE

The intentions behind the online campaign #DontJudge MeChallenge sound positive and empowering, but, in the end, they were anything but. This social media campaign was supposed to show how unkind it is to body shame people on the internet, but it actually ended up doing just the opposite. Young people around the world began taking pictures and videos of themselves and posting them online to Instagram, Twitter, and Vine. In these pictures, they appeared with many artificial and drawn-on flaws, such as acne, unibrows, braces, glasses, pale skin, or missing teeth. Then, one by one, they wipe off these flaws and reveal themselves as relatively attractive. Instead of sending a message that everyone is beautiful in their own ways, this was saying just the opposite. Teens are portraying themselves as "ugly" and then transforming (often with the help of makeup) into someone much more traditionally attractive.

In response to the hypocritical message of #DontJudgeMeChallenge, the #BeautyinAllChallenge was created. This campaign was designed to do what the first one had boasted: encourage people to share, accept, and honor their natural imperfections as a part of who they were. Young people posted images of themselves without makeup or any enhancements. They then added comments showing that they loved and respected exactly who they were. Some of the posts stated,

"I rarely smile, but I have acne, I wear glasses, those things do not step me being beautiful."

"As a trans guy, i'm always insecure about how masculine i look, and i dont really smile in photos bc i feel like it makes me more masc. but despite my insecurities, i'm gonna post this in the #BeautyInAllChallenge bc im gonna love myself today."

"My face gots some bumps, my nails aren't perfect, but I'm still fabulous."

"My body is not yours to feel ashamed of."

Shame often ties into feelings of fear and anxiety, making it much harder to think clearly and make good decisions.

from a store and feels guilty, he will likely say to himself, "I did a rotten thing stealing that shirt. I feel awful about it." However, someone who feels ashamed will more likely say, "I am a terrible person because I stole that shirt." Guilt can be a positive emotion because it often inspires people to right wrongs, or at least decide never to repeat them. Shame, however, just emphasizes to people that they are bad, and so much more prone to repeat negative behavior. Guilt tends to lead directly to change, while shame leads to worsening behavior and increased risk of anything from eating disorders and drug addiction to depression and suicide. In other words, guilt condemns the *behavior*, while shame condemns the *person*.

In an anonymous blog post on LifeTeen.com, a young person described the pain of shame when she wrote, "Shame is a simple word, only five letters, one of those words everyone spells right on a spelling test without needing to study. In my life, however, shame has not been simple. Shame is an ice-cold hand, clutching at my heart, grabbing my face and forcing me to look at who I used to be and what I have done. It uses its cold, sharp fingers to point to each individual mistake, hissing questions and accusations into my ears that are all too eager to hear them."

There is no doubt that shame hurts and damages, but what can be done to combat it? Is it a life sentence? No—there are solutions and ways to deal with shame.

A NEW MEDIUM FOR AN OLD BEHAVIOR

One person who educates others about the ramifications of internet shaming and teens is Rebecca "Kiki" Weingarten M.Sc. Ed, MFA. An Education, Tech, and Tech-Life coach, she is the former director of Youth Services with the Bloomberg administration in New York City. Today she works with parents, educators, and teens on issues in education, performance, tech, psychology, and mental health. "Online is a new medium for doing something that has been going on since the beginning of time," she explained in an interview with the author. "It can serve as a way to develop an 'us and them' mentality. Everyone wants to be in the right group as they find their place in the world. One way people do this is to stand opposite, look at someone else, judge them and say they aren't 'like us,' they don't measure up." She emphasized that the internet makes that easier than ever to do. "You are anonymous and invisible behind a keyboard," she said. "You can say and throw out whatever you want and not have to look at the person's face, deal with their feelings or deal with the ramifications of what you've done on a human level. The problem is, once words or an image is out there, you have completely lost control of it," she added.

Weingarten gave the example of a client who gave her twelve-year-old daughter a smartphone. She and some friends had a party, got drunk, and someone videoed it

and put it online. "Kids believe there are no repercussions to this," said Weingarten, "but there are lots of repercussions on a personal level by shaming or stigmatizing the child; educationally it can effect college applications one day, and more." She also warns that there are many other results from shaming, including in some cases leading to depression and, as we've read in the news, even suicide. "These shaming experiences can be brutal," she added. "These issues can be lasting, affect their present and future lives, and most teens just don't comprehend this."

To help prevent the pain of internet shaming, both teens and their parents have important responsibilities, Weingarten stressed. "Parents need to talk to their kids about technology and behavior. They should consider writing out a contract with their kids before the kids get a smartphone. Kids have grown up with these phones and the Internet—they don't know anything else," Weingarten stated. "They have to learn to balance high TECH with high TOUCH or emotional skills." In addition, she emphasized that parents should spend as much time discussing the ideas of empathy, kindness, and compassion as anything else. "It is essential to keep lines of communication open between parents and young people," she added. "Kids need to feel they have someone they can talk to, and that they can turn to their parents for support." Weingarten also recommended that schools

Sitting at a keyboard, a person can be anything and anyone he or she wants to be. This anonymity can lead someone to be unkind or unthinking.

HELPING A FRIEND

How can you help a friend who has been shamed on the internet? It will change from one situation to the next, of course, but here are some general ideas to help get started:

- Listen to them as they go through the emotions of shame, anger, and depression.
- Encourage them to confide in someone they trust for help and guidance.
- Talk to friends and classmates about not sharing or forwarding the embarrassing information to others.
- Get help immediately if there is any indication the person has become suicidal.
- Remind them that they are not alone in this situation and that, over time, it will get better.
- Stress how important the person is and how much they mean to a variety of people.
- Help connect the person with local, state, and national resources that can offer help.
- Validate the person's emotions, letting them know that they are normal and expected.

Finally, heed the words of Sue Scheff, parent and author of *Google Bomb: The Untold Story of the $11.3M Verdict that Changed the Way We Use the Internet.* She wrote for HuffPost Parents, "Digital shaming is not caused by the Internet. It's human behavior. We must start by being accountable for our own keystrokes, as well as being a proactive digital warrior. If you see someone being cyberslammed online, reach out with a virtual hug or kind word," she advised. "It can be a very lonely when you are being digitally demolished. The fear is real. The hopelessness can be overwhelming. But there are also so many kind people online that can be there for you. Being a digital upstander," she added, "is as important as being a good neighbor."

Helping someone who has been internet shamed is like comforting them after any type of crisis. Be willing to stand up for your friend in whatever way needed.

get actively involved in preventing internet shaming issues. "They should have assemblies, plus put measures and rules in place."

What happens when a student is shamed? "If you don't have a parent or guardian you're comfortable confiding in, turn to an older friend, even just an older teen, or a favorite teacher, church leader, a coach, librarian, school counselor—any adult you feel close to and trust—and ask for help," she encouraged. "Gather your resources and your adult support—but do it. Get the support. There are people out there who care about you and want to help."

PREVENTING THE SHAME

Just as it is impossible to guarantee you won't ever be in a car accident if you drive safely (there are all those other careless drivers out there!), it is impossible to guarantee you won't ever be shamed on the internet even if you do everything right. However, there are some common sense precautions that can be taken.

1. Think very, very carefully before posting anything about yourself—a comment, a photo, or a video. Ask yourself: will this hurt someone's reputation? Can this offend someone? Will I want a future

One of the most important things to remember when posting on any kind of social media is to think first. What possible ramifications could that post have?

employer seeing this post? Whenever you post something on the internet, you are creating a "digital footprint" that is almost impossible to erase.

2. Think very, very carefully before sharing anything that someone sent to you. Ask yourself the same questions. Remember that every person in that photo or video is a human being with feelings. Is sending the image or making a comment worth hurting that person? Would you do the same thing if face to face? Never post any image of a person you know without his or her express consent to do so. According to writer

Remember that once you post anything—text, photographs, or videos—on the internet, you can never completely erase it. Think carefully before you post.

Hayah Eichler-Goldlist, writer for *The Jerusalem Post*, Dr. Gilad Ravid, researcher of social networks once said, "When we share or re-tweet, we need to understand that we are now part of the process."

3. Remember that cameras are truly everywhere in today's world. A camera is in every pocket and purse wherever you go. And, within seconds, that picture your friend took can be online—and from there, it is unstoppable. If you're going to go to a party, out on a date, or anywhere else where you might want an element of privacy because of your actions, then don't drink or use drugs that will allow you to forget about those cameras. As Jon Ronson wrote in his book, *So You've Been Shamed on the Internet,* "We are creating a world where the smartest way to survive is to be bland."

4. Don't trust people easily. Often the photos and videos on the internet were uploaded by boy/girlfriends, best friends, classmates, and even family members. It is not uncommon for someone to do this not to shame or hurt someone, but to be funny—so make it clear to everyone you know that an embarrassing image uploaded to the endless World Wide Web is *not* funny.

WHEN IT'S TOO LATE

You took precautions. You were careful. But, in the end, a private image of you has been put on the internet, or a comment you made has been completely misunderstood.

Regardless of the particular circumstances, you are now being shamed online. Now what? Unlike celebrities and wealthy CEOs, you don't have a public relations firm or a fleet of managers to help dampen the flames of the scandal.

First, find someone to help you. Don't hide what is happening, as that will only make the situation worse, and compound those feelings of shame and embarrassment. Who do you know and trust? It can be at home—your parents, a sibling or older teen. It could be at school—a teacher, librarian, coach, counselor or other faculty member. It could be at work—an employer or coworker. It could be from within the community—a friend, church leader, business owner, or other mentor. Just find someone and explain what happened.

Second, remember that as global as the internet is, it is also just as fleeting. Social media stories come and go at lightning speeds, so, chances are, your moment of humiliation will be buried far faster than you had imagined. It also helps to remember that just because something is on the internet, does not mean it is true. Remind people of that. As Dr. Ravid stated, "We're used to consuming traditional media. We now have a natural tendency to think that everything we read is true. If it's written, it must have happened."

Third, keep the event in perspective. Naturally, it feels *huge* right now, almost insurmountable. You will never, ever get past it—except you will. Think about what you were embarrassed about a few years ago. Remember how it all blew over and you went on, despite how you felt at the time? This will be the same. Wounds heal with time.

Fourth, do your utmost best not to feel ashamed. That is easier said than done, of course. But remember that everyone makes mistakes—yours just happened to get caught. Admit you did whatever it was ("You're right, I said something incredibly stupid" or "Yup, that was me dancing in my underwear in the parking lot last night") and you take the fuel out of the scandal far more quickly.

Fifth, ask the person who originally posted the images of you to remove them as soon as possible. Ask anyone who might have forwarded the images to do the same.

Finally, take a moment to forgive yourself for being human and fallible. Feel guilty rather than ashamed, and then learn from what happened and resolve not to let it happen again.

If the shaming incident does not blow over quickly and has the potential to affect your life in more permanent ways, these steps are not enough. In these incidences, families must sometimes reach out for legal assistance and find a way to end the shaming within the courtroom.

Being shamed online is painful, but it does not have to be lethal.

CHAPTER 5

Fifteen-year-old Quandria Bryant's father Donnell forced her to carry a sign outside her school that read, "I have a bad attitude and am disrespectful to people who try to help me." Quandria's crime? She was disrespectful to her teachers.

Thirteen year-old Ava Abbott's mother accessed her daughter's Facebook page and replaced her picture with one of her wearing a big red X. Mrs. Abbott added, "I do not know how to keep my [mouth shut]. I am no longer allowed on Facebook or my phone." Ava's crime? She was disrespectful to her mother.

Eighteen-year-old Melissa King was crowned Miss Teen Delaware in 2013. When someone pointed out that she had been in a pornographic movie as a young and desperate teen, news spread fast. In the end, King had to give up her crown, while online she was slut shamed.

Whether or not any of these teens learned to change their behavior by being shamed in public is up for debate. Images of all three were certainly repeatedly played on the local news, as well as all over the internet. What began as a

single post turned into a worldwide indictment for complete strangers to see and comment on.

Internet shaming is a part of today's culture, from a way to punish kids or embarrass celebrities to an anonymous way to point fingers at people's errors in judgments or simple mistakes. What can be done to stop this modern method of punishment from affecting your life?

AT THE LOCAL LEVEL

Even though internet shaming is a global issue, it can be attacked at a local level. Starting with your school or your community is often the best way to affect the people around you. Some possible activities to implement in your area include the following:

• Writing a letter about the problems and ramifications of internet shaming for your school newspaper or other publication (in print or online).
• Creating handouts to be used in the counselor's offices or given directly to students.
• Inviting speakers and local organization representatives to discuss the impact of internet shaming.
• Creating a petition for local families, parents, faculty, and students to sign.

Melissa King resigned her position as Miss Teen Delaware and was given a year of probation. It was the online shaming that was the hardest to bear.

Asking teachers to bring in and implement anti-bullying videos and other resources is an option, as internet shaming is a type of bullying. According to Goldlist-Eichler, as Orna Hellinger, director of the Center for Safe Internet stated in a national press release, "We see no difference between cyberbullying and shaming; both are dangerous, both make cynical use of the Internet and adversely take advantage of its power. . . . online offenses are no less destructive than any other case of violence and sometimes even more so—the speed at which a person is brought to trial in the town square, without the users knowing

Speaking out against issues like internet shaming is one way a single person can make a difference in the world.

or recognizing the full picture is dangerous, both for those involved and their surroundings."

AT A WIDER LEVEL

Of course, making larger changes in how internet shaming is handled in today's culture is also extremely important. To do this, you can:

• Write letters to senators and other representatives about the need for internet shaming legislation.
• Create an online petition and garner as many signatures as possible. Then send the petition to the attention of state and national representatives.
• Post comments to your favorite websites asking if they have it in their terms of service to remove any photos or videos of people in graphic situations. If they don't, start a campaign of online users to encourage the site to do so.

OTHER POSSIBLE SOLUTIONS

A number of websites will remove videos that they perceive as "inappropriate" or that violate their terms of service. Some experts believe that, in addition to these steps, the websites should report these videos to the police or Child Protective Services, depending on the subject matter.

Jonathan Zittrain, an American professor of internet law and author of *The Future of the Internet—And*

How to Stop It, suggested a different solution to internet shaming. He told Whitney Phillips and Kate Miltner of The Awl that "Twitter users could be given the option to update or retract 'bad' information, which would then ping everyone who interacted with the original tweet. Existing damage would thus be mitigated . . ."

GATHERING RESOURCES

If you or someone you know has been shamed online, it is important that you find help wherever possible. One of the ways to do this is carefully analyze what kind of behavior, if any, led to the shame issue. If pictures were taken because you over indulged in alcohol or drugs, for example, it can helpful to connect with organizations specifically geared to help young people with substance abuse issues. If you are being bullied into posing for photos or participating in sexual activities, many national anti-bullying groups can help. If you are in a family situation that is dangerous and carries risk of being hurt, Child Protective Services can step in.

There are a many different organizations and associations online to help deal with online shaming. One is called Bystander Revolution (www.bystanderrevolution.org). It has more than three hundred one-to-two minute videos posted by actors such as Ansel Elgort and Nina Dobrev, as well as students and leaders about dealing with cyberbullying and many other problems. Bystander Revolution was founded in 2014 by MacKenzie Besoz, an author and mother. She wanted to

CREATING AN ANTI-SHAMING EVENT

Raising awareness of how internet shaming can affect people's lives is important for everyone, and one way to do that is to organize some type of anti-shaming event for school. Here are a few ideas on how to get started:

- Host an app competition: Hold a contest at school to see which student/class can create the most innovative and effective anti-shaming app.
- Focus on diversity: Hold a talent show that allows students to demonstrate their talents.
- Create an anti-shaming policy for the school: Write a policy to cover what should be done if a student gets involved in or is hurt by any type of internet shaming.
- Get involved with National Bullying Prevention Month and all of the activities they offer. (Check it out at www. stompoutbullying.org.)
- Host a community event: Invite parents and other concerned citizens to a program explaining internet shaming and how it can be prevented and reported.
- Create wristbands/t-shirts: Contact a local company to produce wristbands or t-shirts and sell them as a school fundraiser or hand out at anti-internet shaming rallies or events.

create a site that would provide "direct, peer-to-peer advice about practical things individuals can do to help defuse bullying." The site's motto is "Simple acts of kindness, courage, and inclusion anyone can use to take the power out of bullying."

A SIX-EPISODE WARNING TALE

One way you can be sure that internet shaming is becoming a bigger and bigger problem in today's world is when the subject gets its own television show. In 2016, the Syfy channel presented a six-episode series titled "The Internet Ruined My Life." Each episode is thirty minutes long and carefully explains how a single post can result in disaster.

"Social media has made our lives easier and connected people, but there's another side: These are warnings," stated Heather Olander, Syfy's senior vice president of development and production in an article by Susan Karlin. "Hopefully parents will watch this show with their kids. Younger users are less private and live their lives more in the public, so they don't think about the consequences so much as the older users. Anonymity enables threats that you'd never make in person. . . We hope that shining light on this issue will start a discussion and raise awareness to effect change," she added.

Events like talent shows give students the chance to see what their peers can do well and, perhaps, create a new connection or friendship.

Episodes have looked at a variety of kinds of online shamings. One episode focused on Leigh van Bryan, a visitor from England who happened to use the slang term "destroy" instead of "party" in one of his tweets. "Free this week, for quick gossip/prep before I go and destroy America?" he posted. Van Bryan was looking forward to exploring Los Angeles with a friend when the Department of Homeland Security detained him at the L.A. airport by in early 2012.

Van Bryan was handcuffed and tossed into a cell with drug dealers for twelve hours. His passport was confiscated, his luggage was searched, and he was interrogated on exactly what plans he had in mind to hurt the United States. "The officials told us we were not allowed in to the country because of Leigh's tweet," explained his friend Emily Banting. "They asked me why we wanted to destroy America, and we tried to explain it meant to . . . party." The two visitors were returned to the airport the following day and put on a plane back to Europe. "It's just so ridiculous it's almost funny, but at the time it was really scary," stated van Bryan. "The Homeland Security agents were treating me like some kind of terrorist." Neither Bunting nor van Bryan will be allowed to return to the United States until they apply for new visas.

"The Internet Ruined My Life" emphasizes that the legal world is lagging behind the online one. Laws to

It is easy to feel guilty for making mistakes, but it is much more effective to think about your actions and figure out how you can do better in the future.

THE TYLER CLEMENTI FOUNDATION/INSTITUTE FOR CYBERSAFETY

Tyler Clementi was one unusual guy. He played the violin and rode a unicycle, often practicing those two skills simultaneously. After graduating from high school, he enrolled in Rutgers University and his skill on the violin quickly earned him a seat in the college's orchestra.

While at college, Clementi's new roommate set up a web cam without telling him. He used it to film Clementi kissing another male college student. The video went onto the net and soon people were posting rude comments that Clementi saw. On the evening of Saturday, September 22, 2010, the eighteen-year-old posted on Facebook saying, "Jumping off the G.W. Bridge—sorry." Hours later, his body was found in the Hudson River.

Clementi's roommate, Dharun Ravi, was sentenced to thirty days in jail and three years' probation, along with three hundred hours of community service. In addition, he has to pay a $10,000 fine which will be sent to the victims of bias and hate crimes. As the judge in the case stated to the Associated Press for *The Washington Post*, "I do not believe he [Ravi] hated Tyler Clementi. He had no reason to, but I do believe he acted out of colossal insensitivity."

To cope with their loss and to try and prevent other families for going through anything similar, the Clementi family and the New York Law School established the Tyler Clementi Foundation/Institute for Cybersafety. "What we're trying to do is end online and offline bullying—in schools, workplaces, and faith communities," Sean Kosofky, the head of the foundation, told Daniel Hubbard of The Patch.

The foundation invites people of all ages to come to their website and sign their pledge about the pain and danger of internet shaming. The pledge urges everyone to be an "upstander" who does not just sit passively when

Jane and Joseph Clementi stay active in social circles to continue to remind people of the dangers of cyberbullying.

seeing bullying of any kind, but to stand up and object. More than a thousand people have signed it so far. In part, the pledge states the following:

- I pledge to become an Upstander by standing up to bullying whether I'm at school, at home, at work, in my house of worship, or out with friends, family, colleagues, or teammates.
- I will work to make others feel safe and included by treating them with respect and compassion.
- I will not use insulting or demeaning language, slurs, gestures, facial expressions, or jokes, about anyone's sexuality, size, gender, race, any kind of disability, religion, class, politics, or other differences in person or while using technology.
- I will state my disagreement or discomfort about people's differences in ways that are respectful rather than insulting or demeaning.
- I will encourage my peers, family members, and colleagues to do the same and will speak up when they use prejudiced language about any group for any reason.

The rest of the pledge can be found at http://www.tylerclementi.org/pledge.

STEPS:	FACEBOOK
	1. Report/remove the tag.
	2. Ask a friend to remove it.
	3. Send an email to info@support.facebook.com.
	4. Submit a complaint via the Facebook Intellectual Property Infringement form.
	5. Post in the Help community and get advice from other users and Facebook staff.
	6. Submit a complaint via the Facebook Terms Violation Reporting Form.

STEPS:	INSTAGRAM
	1. Select "Hide from My Profile" to de-tag.
	2. Choose "More Options."
	3. Choose "Remove Me from Photo."
	4. Report photo as inappropriate.

	TWITTER
STEPS:	1. Access http://support.twitter.com/ forms/abusiveuser.
	2. Select the relevant option, i.e. "I am being directly mentioned."
	3. Fill out the relevant form and submit a report to Twitter.

protect people from shaming and other types of harassment simply do not exist yet. Ari Ezra Waldman, a New York Law School associate professor stated that "too many judges and juries dismiss the online world as not real, and online harassment as just words. Too many young people are growing up not knowing what is appropriate and not with technology. We need to train school administrators, parents, and children starting in elementary school how to behave online and take privacy seriously, and give lawyers the tools to represent these kinds of clients."

REMOVING THOSE PHOTOS!

According to recent polls and surveys, one in ten social media users has posted content they regretted sharing. Twenty-nine percent of Facebook users report being humiliated by the embarrassing content their friends have posted about them. Ten percent of teens report being victimized by others posting unflattering pictures without the teens' consent.

Just how difficult is it to actually remove these types of posts from different social media sites? Each site is slightly different, but here are the steps for several of the primary sites.

Remember, of course, that while these processes will remove the original post or photos, once they have been shared and sent on, it is virtually impossible to ensure all copies are no longer online. As the saying goes, "The Internet is forever."

Being shamed for anything is an awful experience. It hurts now—and it can keep hurting. Misunderstood words, vulnerable images, and exposed photos, whether you are aware of them or not, can haunt you, especially now that the potential audience is the entire world, rather than just the people who happen to be nearby. Internet shaming has driven many young people to drastic measures that they cannot undo. It has made them feel desperate and worried and very alone—but it does not have to. Internet shaming is unpleasant, but it is not permanent. Knowing that you are not alone, that there are answers and solutions and that (like everything else that flits across the internet and then disappears) this moment will pass, can help.

Take those common sense steps to make sure that you are never shamed on the internet. Share the information with your friends, school, and community so they can take those steps too. And then, if you are shamed online, step back, take a deep breath and know that you will survive this.

GLOSSARY

admonish To scold, warn, or advise someone.

catalyst A substance that works as a stimulus to change.

child protective services A government agency that responds to reports of child abuse or neglect.

commiserate To sympathize with or feel pity.

derogatory Displaying an attitude that is critical or insulting.

disparage To discredit or belittle someone or something.

don To put on, such as clothing.

enhancements Improvements or extras, such as in quality.

fallible Liable to be wrong or misleading.

flippant An attitude that is offhand or casual, not serious.

fodder Material for causing a kind of response.

indictment A formal type of accusation or charge.

nuance A fine difference in meaning or expression.

pornography Sexually explicit printed or visual material.

Puritan A strict belief system, often referring to the late sixteenth and seventeenth centuries.

settlement An official or court-ordered agreement.

stance The position or attitude of a person or organization.

vigilante A citizen who punishes lawbreakers.

vilify To speak or write ill of or slander.

vulnerable At risk of being damaged or hurt.

FOR MORE INFORMATION

Megan Meier Foundation
515 Jefferson St. Suite A
St. Charles, MO 63301
(636) 757-3501
Website: www.meganmeierfoundation.org/

The Megan Meier Foundation is dedicated to a young girl who committed suicide after being targeted and taunted online. It offers multiple resources for schools, plus a list of the events it hosts each year to fight bullying and cyberbullying.

Internet Keep Safe Coalition Headquarters
97 S. Second St. 100 #244
San Jose, CA 95113
(703) 717-9066
Website: ikeepsafe.org/

Established in 2005, iKeepSafe's mission is to "see generations of the world's children grow up safely using technology and the Internet."

Stop Bullying.gov
US Department of Health and Human Services
200 Independence Ave. S.W.
Washington, DC 20201
Website: www.stopbullying.gov/

This government site provides information on different types of bullying, who is most at risk, and how to prevent and respond to bullying situations.

End to Cyber Bullying Organization (ETCB)
147 W. 35th St. Suite 1404
New York, NY 10001
Website: www.endcyberbullying.org/

ETCB was first established in 2011 and aims to "raise awareness and provide a plethora of cyberbullying information, offer compassionate, approachable services, and mobilize students, educators, parents, and others in taking efforts to end cyberbullying."

Hey UGLY Inc. NFP
PO Box 345
Rolling Prairie, IN 465371
(219) 778-2011
Website: www.heyugly.org

Hey UGLY (Unique Gifted Lovable You) is a group dedicated to giving young people the tools they need to empower them and "to be part of the solution to societal ills like bullying."

The Cybersmile Foundation
530 Lytton Ave. 2nd Floor
Palo Alto, CA 94301
(650) 617-3474
Website: www.cybersmile.org/

The Cybersmile Organization focuses on making sure that people can be a part of the digital world "without suffering abuse, harassment, or intimidation."

NOVA
510 King St. Suite 424
Alexandria, VA 22314
(800) 879-6682
Website: www.trynova.org/

NOVA stands for National Organization for Victim Assistance. It emphasizes assistance for anyone who has been harmed by crime or any other kind of crisis.

EIE

PO Box 1532

Great Falls, VA 22066

(888) 744-0004

Website: www.enough.org/

Enough is Enough focuses on keeping the internet safe for children and families. It focuses on the problems of child stalking, child pornography, and sexual predation.

National Center for Missing and Exploited Children

Charles B. Wang International Children's Building

699 Prince St.

Alexandria, VA 22314-3175

(866) 411-5437

Website:www.netsmartz.org/

The National Center for Missing and Exploited Children offers a site about online safety called Netsmartz. It has separate sections for kids and teens.

Center for Innovative Public Health Research

555 N. El Camino Real #A347

San Clemente, CA 92672-6745

(877) 302-6858

Website: innovativepublichealth.org/

CiPHR's motto is "decoding how technology influences and can improve public health." They offer a great deal of information about how the internet affects the mental health and well-being of young people.

WEBSITES

Because of the changing nature of internet links, Rosen Publishing has developed an online list of websites related to the subject of this book. This site is updated regularly. Please use this link to access the list:

http://www.rosenlinks.com/411/shame

FOR FURTHER READING

Bazelon, Emily. *Sticks and Stones: Defeating the Culture of Bullying and Rediscovering the Power of Character and Empathy.* New York, NY: Random House, 2014.

Hamilton, Tracy Brown. *Combatting Internet Shaming.* New York, NY: Rosen Young Adult, 2016.

Harasymlw, Therese. *Cyberbullying and the Law.* New York, NY: Rosen Central, 2012.

Hinduja, Sameer. *Bullying Beyond the Schoolyard: Preventing and Responding to Cyberbullying.* Newbury Park, CA: Corwin, 2008.

Hunter, Nick. *Cyber Bullying.* Portsmouth, NH: Heinemann, 2011.

Ivester, Matt. *lol . . .OMG! What Every Student Needs to Know about Online Reputation Management, Digital Citizenship, and Cyberbullying.* San Francisco, CA: Serra Knight Publishing, 2012.

Jacobs, Thomas A. *Teen Cyberbullying Investigated: Where Do Your Rights End and Consequences Begin?* Golden Valley, MN: Free Spirit Publishing, 2010.

Jacquet, Jennifer. *Is Shame Necessary?* New York, NY: Pantheon Books, 2015.

Lindeen, Mary. *Digital Safety Smarts: Preventing Cyberbullying.* Minneapolis, MN: Lerner Classroom, 2016.

Lohmann, Raychelle Cassada. *The Bullying Workbook for Teens: Activities to Help You Deal with Social*

Aggression and Cyberbullying. Oakland, CA: Instant Help, 2013.

MacEachern, Robyn. *Cyberbullying: Deal with It and Ctrl Alt Delete It.* Toronto, Canada: James Lorimer, 2011.

Peterson, Judy Monroe. *How to Beat Cyberbullying.* New York, NY: Rosen Central, 2012.

Raatma, Lucia. *Cyberbullying.* New York, NY: Scholastic. 2013.

Roberts, Walter. *Bullying from Both Sides.* Newbury Park, CA: Corwin, 2005.

Rogers, Vanessa. *Cyberbullying: Activities to Help Children and Teens to Stay Safe in a Texting, Twittering, Social Networking World.* London, England: Jessica Kingsley Publishers, 2010.

Ronson, Jon. *So You've Been Publicly Shamed.* New York, NY: Riverhead Books, 2015.

Schwartz, Heather. *Cyberbullying.* North Mankato, MN: Capstone Press, 2013.

Spivet, Bonnie. *Stopping Cyberbullying.* New York, NY: Powerkids Press, 2012.

Ster, Caroline Rose. *Face 2 Face: Navigating through Cyberbullying, Peer Abuse, and Bullying.* Lake City, CO: Western Reflections Publishing, 2011.

Tannenbaum, Leora. *I Am Not a Slut: Slut-Shaming in the Age of the Internet.* New York, NY: Harper Perennial Books, 2015.

BIBLIOGRAPHY

Associated Press. "Dharun Ravi Sentence in Rutgers Webcam Case Renews Hate Crime Law Debate.' The Washington Post. May 22, 2012. https://www.washingtonpost.com/national/dharun-ravi-sentence-in-rutgers-webcam-case-renews-hate-crime-law-debate/2012/05/22/gIQAui0DiU_story.html.

Audrie Pott Foundation. Retrieved April 12, 2016 (http://blog.audriepottfoundation.com/).

Bennett, Robbyn Peters. "Parents are Losing It on Social Media and Shaming Children." Seattle Times. August 22,2015.http://www.seattletimes.com/opinion/parents-are-losing-it-on-social-media-and-shaming-children.

Brito, Jerry. "'We Do It for the Lulz': What Makes LulzSec Tick?" Time. June 17, 2011. techland.time.com/2011/06/17/we-do-it-for-the-lulz-what-makes-lulzsec-tick/2/.

Buxton, Ryan. "Tommy Jordan, Dad Who Shot Daughter's Laptop, Says He Doesn't Regret It." HuffPost Live. April 3, 2014. http://www.huffingtonpost.com/2014/04/03/tommy-jordan-shot-daughters-laptop_n_5071661.html.

Bystander Revolution. 2015. http://www.bystanderrevolution.org/about.

Cunnion, Jeannie. "Punishment and Discipline: Why They Have Nothing in Common." Fox News Opinion. October 2, 2014. http://www.foxnews

.com/opinion/2014/10/02/punishment-and-discipline-why-have-nothing-in-common.html.

Diaz, Joseph and Lauren Effron. "Former CFO on Food Stamps after Controversial Viral Video about Chick-Fil-A." ABC News. March 25, 2015. http://abcnews.go.com/Business/cfo-food-stamps-controversial-viral-video/story?id=29533695.

Eccles, Louise and Claire Ellicott. "Girl, 13 Stood on Ledge and Begged Boy to Delete Sex Video from Phone . . . Then She Fell 60 Feet to her Death." Daily Mail. January 16, 2013 http://www.dailymail.co.uk/news/article-2263452/Girl-13-stood-ledge-begged-boy-delete-sex-video-phone--fell-60ft-death.html.

Eichler-Goldlist, Hayah. "In Wake of Suicide, Social Media Expert Calls for Comparisons When Posting Online." The Jerusalem Post. May 25, 2015. http://www.jpost.com/Israel-News/In-wake-of-suicide-social-media-expert-calls-for-compassion-when-posting-online-404040.

Engel, Beverly. "The Power of Apology." Psychology Today. July 1, 2002. https://www.psychologytoday.com/articles/200208/the-power-apology?collection=93010.

Engel, Beverly. *The Power of Apology: Healing Steps to Transform All Your Relationships*. New York, NY: Wiley, 2002.

Fallon, Claire. "Jon Ronson Shames Shamers in 'So You Think You've Been Publicly Shamed,'." Huffington Post. March 25, 2015. http://www.huffingtonpost.com/2015/03/25/jon-ronson-wants-us-all-t_n_6935060.html.

France, Lisa. "No! Don't Share This Stuff Online!" CNN. Retrieved April 3, 2016 http://www.cnn.com/videos/tech/2015/01/20/fake-stories-internet-psa-lisas-desk-orig-mg.cnn.

Hubbard, Daniel. "Tyler Clementi's Parents Launch New Campaign To End Bullying." The Patch. June 16, 2015. http://patch.com/new-jersey/ridgewood/tyler-clementis-parents-launch-new-campaign-end-bullying.

Judah, Sam. "Is it OK to Humiliate Your Child Online?" BBC Trending. June 8, 2015. http://www.bbc.com/news/blogs-trending-33023129.

Goodman, Amy. "'Audrie & Daisy': Mother of Audrie Pott, Teen Who Committed Suicide after Assault, Tells Her Story." Independent Global News. January 29, 2016. http://www.democracynow.org/2016/1/29/audrie_daisy_mother_of_audrie_pott.

Gray, Joslyn. "Shocking or Brilliant? 11 Examples of Public Shaming as Punishment." Babble. Retrieved April 6, 2016. http://www.babble.com/mom/shocking-or-brilliant-11-examples-of-public-shaming-as-punishment.

Hartley-Parkinson, Richard. "'I'm Going to Destroy America and Dig up Marilyn Monroe': British Pair Arrested in U.S. on Terror Charges over Twitter Jokes." Daily Mail. January 31, 2012. http://www.dailymail.co.uk/news/article-2093796/Emily-Bunting-Leigh-Van-Bryan-UK-tourists-arrested-destroy-America-Twitter-jokes.html.

Harwood, Erika. "These 13 Inspiring Tweets Totally Take Down the 'Don't Judge Challenge.'" MTV. July

8,2015.http://www.mtv.com/news/2207124/beauty-in-all-challenge/.

"How to Remove your Embarrassing Photos from Social Media." Who Is Hosting This? Retrieved April 13, 2016. http://www.whoishostingthis.com/blog/2014/09/16/remove-photos/.

"How to Slap Shame in the Face." LifeTeen.com. Retrieved April 14, 2016. http://lifeteen.com/blog/slap-shame-face/.

Karlin, Susan. "Syfy's 'The Internet Ruined my Life' is a Cautionary Tale in Cyberbullying." CoCreate. March 9, 2016. http://www.fastcocreate.com/3057523/syfys-the-internet-ruined-my-life-is-a-cautionary-tale-in-cyber-bullying.

Lamia, Mary C. Ph.D. "Shame: A Concealed, Contagious, and Dangerous Emotion." Psychology Today. April 4, 2011. https://www.psychologytoday.com/blog/intense-emotions-and-strong-feelings/201104/shame-concealed-contagious-and-dangerous-emotion.

Lowin, Rebekah. "#EndShame Movement asks Parents to Rethink Humiliating Posts about Kids." Today. September 2, 2015. http://www.today.com/parents/endshame-movement-urges-parents-stop-using-internet-disciplinary-tool-t41801.

McNeal, Stephanie. "A Mom Publicly Shamed her 13-Year-Old Daughter for Posing in a Bra on Facebook." Buzzfeed News. May 21, 2015. http://www.buzzfeed.com/stephaniemcneal/mom-calls-out-secret-facebook#.phXql9jva5.

Miller, Michael. "'I Could Have Lost My Life, Too,' says Driver Hit by 'Shamed' Girl Who Jumped from

Bridge." The Washington Post. June 8, 2015. https://www.washingtonpost.com/news/morning-mix/wp/2015/06/08/i-could-have-died-too-says-driver-hit-by-shamed-girl-who-jumped-from-bridge/.

Newman, Jared. "Survey: Most hackers do it for the lulz." PCWorld. August 14, 2014. www.pcworld.com/article/2465209/survey-most-hackers-do-it-for-the-lulz.html.

NPR Staff, "'Publicly Shamed:' Who Needs the Pillory When We've Got Twitter?" NPR. March 31, 2015. http://www.npr.org/2015/03/31/396413638/publicly-shamed-who-needs-the-pillory-when-weve-got-twitter.

Norman, Natasha. "Here's the Truth Behind that Viral Story of a Girl Who Died by Suicide because of Her Dad." News.Mic. June 11, 2015. http://mic.com/articles/120525/here-s-the-truth-behind-that-viral-story-of-a-girl-committing-suicide-because-of-her-dad#.VRe3puMtz.

Phillips, Whitney and Kate Miltner. "The Internet's Vigilante Shame Army." The Awl. December 19, 2012. http://www.theawl.com/2012/12/the-internets-vigilante-shame-army).

"Remembering Tyler Clementi." CBS News. June 7, 2015. http://www.cbsnews.com/news/remembering-tyler-clementi/3/.

Ronson, Jon. "How One Stupid Tweet Blew Up Justice Sacco's Life." The New York Times Magazine. February 12, 2015. http://www.nytimes.com/2015/02/15/magazine/how-one-stupid-tweet-ruined-justine-saccos-life.html.

Ronson, Jon. "How a Tweet Can Ruin Your Life." Esquire. March 4, 2015. http://www.esquire.co.uk/culture/news/a7933/exclusive-extract-from-jon-ronson-book-so-youve-been-publicly-shamed/.

Ronson, Jon. "'Overnight, Everything I Loved Was Gone': The Internet Shaming of Lindsey Stone." The Guardian. February 22, 2015. https://www.theguardian.com/technology/2015/feb/21/internet-shaming-lindsey-stone-jon-ronson.

Ronson, Jon. *So You've Been Publicly Shamed.* New York, NY: Riverhead Books, 2015.

Scheff, Sue. "Digital Shaming: You are Only a Click Away." HuffPost Parents. April 12, 2016. http://www.huffingtonpost.com/sue-scheff/digital-shaming-you-are-only-a-click-away_b_9649264.html.

Schrobsdorff, Susanna. "When Parents Publicly Shame their Kids." Time. June 25, 2015 http://time.com/3935308/when-parents-publicly-shame-their-kids/.

Schwartz, Mattathias. "The Trolls Among Us." New York Times Magazine. August 3, 2008. www.nytimes.com/2008/08/03/magazine/03trolls-t.html?_r=0.

Sulek, Julia Prodis. "San Jose: Boys Apologize in Wrongful Death Lawsuit Settlement over Girl's Suicide." April 3, 2015. http://www.mercurynews.com/bay-area-news/ci_27844832/audrie-pott-parents-agree-settlement-civil-lawsuit-over.

"Take the Pledge." The Tyler Clementi Organization. Retrieved April 3, 2016. http://www.tylerclementi.org/pledge.

"The Father that Shot His Daughter's Computer." The Last Psychiatrist. February 22, 2012. http://thelast-psychiatrist.com/2012/02/the_father_that_shot_his_daugh.html.

Tsabary, Dr. Shefali. The Conscious Parent. Vancouver, BC, Canada: Namaste Publishing 2010.

"Tyler Clementi's Deadly Trip." NoBullying.com. December 22, 2015. http://nobullying.com/tyler-clementi/.

Wallace, Kelly. "Teens Spend a 'Mind-Boggling' 9 Hours a Day Using Media, Report Says. CNN. November 3, 2015. http://www.cnn.com/2015/11/03/health/teens-tweens-media-screen-use-report/.

Waterlow, Lucy. "'I Lost My Job, My Reputation, and I'm Not Able to Date Anymore': Former PR Worker Reveals How She Destroyed her Life One Year after Sending 'Racist' Tweet before Trip to Africa." Daily Mail. February 16, 2015. http://www.dailymail.co.uk/femail/article-2955322/Justine-Sacco-reveals-destroyed-life-racist-tweet-trip-Africa.html.

Weiner, Eric. "Jon Ronson Has Nothing to be Ashamed Of, But What about the Rest of Us?" NPR. April 1, 2015. http://www.npr.org/2015/04/01/396384141/jon-ronson-has-nothing-to-be-ashamed-of-but-what-about-the-rest-of-us.

Weingarten, Rebecca "Kiki." Telephone interview with the author, April 8. 2016.

INDEX

About the Author

Tamra Orr is a full-time author living in the Pacific Northwest. After receiving her Bachelor of Science degree in English and Secondary Education from Ball State University, she began writing full-time for students of all ages. She has written more than 450 nonfiction books for children; plus she writes a great deal of educational assessment material for both state and national tests. She has never been shamed online, but as the mother of four young adults, she has spent hours worrying that one of them would be. This book has inspired many important conversations about responsibility, compassion, and common sense. When she is not writing, Orr is camping with her family, reading a book, or writing letters to friends scattered across the globe.

Photo Credits

Designer: Les Kanturek
Editor and Photo Researcher: Heather Moore Niver